SPOTLIGHT
THE AGE OF
REVOLUTION

Michael Gibson

Wayland

SPOTLIGHT ON HISTORY

Spotlight on the Age of Exploration and Discovery
Spotlight on the Age of Revolution
Spotlight on Elizabethan England
Spotlight on the First World War
Spotlight on the Industrial Revolution
Spotlight on Post-War Europe
Spotlight on the Second World War
Spotlight on the Victorians

First published in 1985 by
Wayland (Publishers) Ltd
49 Lansdowne Place, Hove
East Sussex BN3 1HF, England

© Copyright 1985 Wayland (Publishers) Ltd

British Library Cataloguing in Publication Data
Gibson, Michael
Spotlight on the Age of Revolution.—(Spotlight on history)
1. Europe—Politics and government—18th century—Juvenile
literature 2. Europe—Politics and government—1789–1900—
Juvenile literature
I. Title   II. Series
940.2′53   D286
ISBN 0–85078–590–1

Typeset, printed and bound in the UK at
The Bath Press, Avon

CONTENTS

1 THE ANCIEN RÉGIME

For hundreds of years the feudal system dominated Europe. While ordinary people worked in the fields growing crops, the upper classes ruled and defended them. Of course, there were always exceptions to this simple picture: the traders and craftsmen of the towns, for example, never quite fitted in. As the years went by the feudal system gradually changed and then slowly started to break up. Nevertheless, the 'landed interest'—the nobility, the gentry and the yeomen—continued to control society as government ministers and leaders of the armed forces.

Gradually, a new social class, the bourgeoisie or middle class, made up of merchants, industrialists and professional people, began to exercise growing influence on the life of Western Europe. For the time

An image of the feudal system: peasants at work ploughing the fields around their lord's castle.

*As the feudal system began to break up, merchants and other members
of the middle class grew in importance, both economically and socially.*

being, however, they still had to be content to give first place to the
landed interest.

At the bottom of the social pyramid lay the labouring classes, who
were usually poor and sometimes starving. In 1675, the Governor of
Dauphiné in France observed that 'the great majority of the inhabitants
of this province lived during the winter only from acorns and roots,
and now they can be seen eating the grass of the fields and the bark
of the trees.' An Englishman writing about France in the eighteenth
century commented, 'The poor people seem poor indeed; the children
terribly ragged, if possible worse clad than if with no clothes at all;
as to shoes and stockings they are luxuries.'

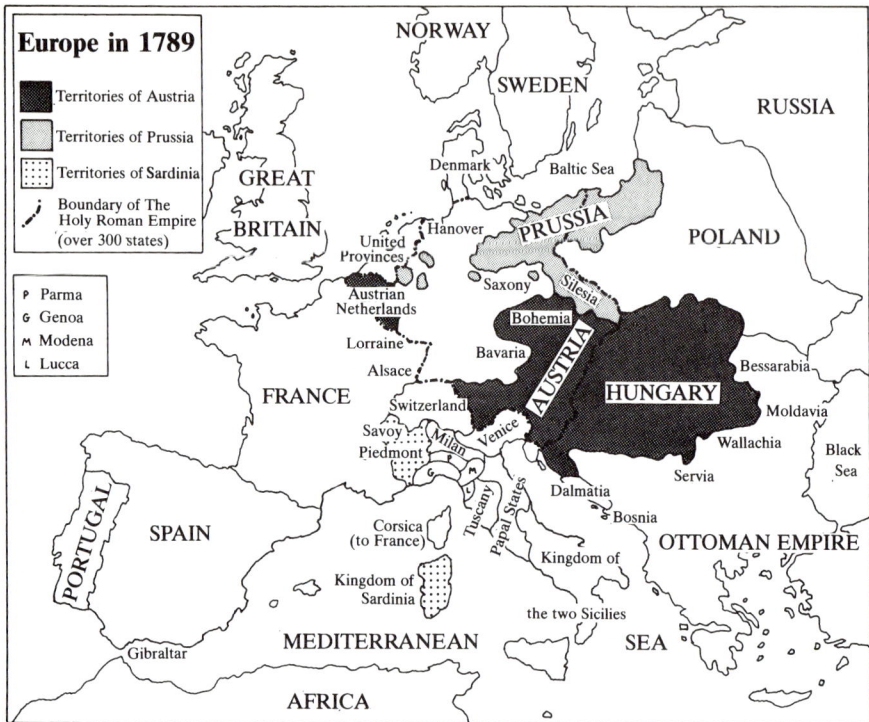

Europe in 1789

- ■ Territories of Austria
- □ Territories of Prussia
- ▦ Territories of Sardinia
- / Boundary of The Holy Roman Empire (over 300 states)

- P Parma
- G Genoa
- M Modena
- L Lucca

NORWAY

SWEDEN

RUSSIA

GREAT BRITAIN

Denmark

Baltic Sea

Hanover

PRUSSIA

POLAND

United Provinces

Saxony

Silesia

Austrian Netherlands

Bohemia

Lorraine

Bavaria

Bessarabia

Alsace

AUSTRIA

HUNGARY

Moldavia

FRANCE

Switzerland

Savoy

Milan

Venice

Wallachia

Black Sea

Piedmont

Servia

Tuscany

Papal States

Dalmatia

Bosnia

PORTUGAL

SPAIN

Corsica (to France)

OTTOMAN EMPIRE

Kingdom of Sardinia

Kingdom of the two Sicilies

Gibraltar

MEDITERRANEAN

SEA

AFRICA

Europe before the start of the French Revolution.

Even though there is a great deal of truth in these statements, they give a very one-sided picture of the labouring classes. The lives of some peasants were improving quite dramatically during the eighteenth century. Indeed, this is probably the reason why labourers dared to voice their complaints. As the historian, Alexander de Tocqueville argued in 1856, revolution occurs not when people are at their lowest but when things are starting to improve and they can see how much better off they could be.

The political scene

During the *ancien régime*, the period before the Age of Revolution, Europe resembled a patchwork quilt of states. France was the richest and most powerful state. The Holy Roman Empire contained Germany, Austria and much of eastern Europe. Prussia had emerged as a great power during the reign of Frederick the Great (1740–86). Russia, too, had added military power to its huge size under Peter the Great (1694–1725) and Catherine the Great (1762–96). The United Provinces (Holland) was a great trading state whose only effective rival was Great Britain. Spain and Portugal had valuable overseas empires as did France, Britain and the United Provinces. Italy was divided into a series of rival states dominated by outside powers. To the east of Europe lay the once-great Ottoman Empire, a mere shadow of its former strength.

Most European states, including France, Austria, Prussia and Russia, were ruled by absolute monarchs, who had the power to make laws and tax their subjects. Great Britain, on the other hand, had a 'constitutional monarchy'; although the King or Queen was head of state, it was Parliament that made the laws and granted taxes. Whatever the form of government, however, ordinary people had to do what they were told.

If the emperors and kings of Europe were safe on their thrones, the Church was less secure. The sixteenth and seventeenth centuries had seen many religious wars, but since that time most people had developed more tolerant attitudes towards faiths other than their own. This new tolerant attitude was one aspect of the philosophical movement known as 'the Enlightenment'. *Philosophes*—French writers like Montesquieu (1689–1755), Voltaire (1694–1778) and Diderot (1713–84)—argued that everything that happened was governed by laws which could be discovered by study and reasoning. These *philosophes* believed that laws and institutions could only be justified if

Voltaire (with arm raised) presides over a meal with other French philosophes, *including Diderot, seated on Voltaire's left.*

The signing of the American Declaration of Independence on 4 July 1776. This document helped to inspire French revolutionaries.

they served a useful purpose. Catherine the Great of Russia wrote: 'What is the true end of monarchy? Not to deprive people of their natural liberty, but to correct their actions, in order to obtain the supreme good.' These ideas proved to be very dangerous as they led to many criticisms of the way in which the European countries were governed and the differences that existed between rich and poor.

The American War of Independence (1775–83) caused great excitement in Europe. At first, it appeared to be just another struggle between the Great Powers: the French and Spanish gave their support to the American colonists in their war with the British, whose power had grown so great that the other European countries were glad of the opportunity to reduce it. The war, however, also gave widespread publicity to the colonists' beliefs as expressed in their Declaration of Independence:

> We hold these truths to be self-evident, that all men are created equal, that they are endowed by their Creator with certain inalienable rights, that among these are Life, Liberty and the Pursuit of Happiness. That to secure these rights, Governments are instituted among Men, deriving their just powers from the consent of the governed. That whenever any Form of Government becomes destructive of these ends, it is the Right of the People to alter or to abolish it, and to institute new government.

8

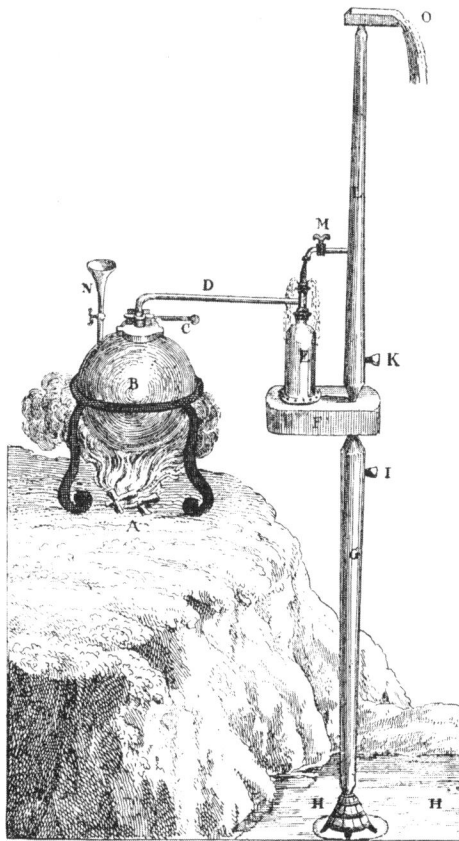

An engraving of Thomas Savery's steam engine of 1698, which was described as 'a new invention for raising of water'.

Scientific revolution

Political, economic and social changes were accompanied by scientific and technological progress. At the beginning of the eighteenth century, power for industrial purposes was still provided by men, water or the wind. The need to drain coal mines of water led to the introduction of the first steam engines by Denis Papin (1647–1712), Thomas Savery (1650–1715) and Thomas Newcomen (1663–1729). European rivers were carefully improved until they became major routes. In England alone, there were 900 miles of navigable river by 1725. As far back as 1662, Charles II of England had provided the Royal Society with its charter. This famous institution included among its early members Isaac Newton who revolutionized science by developing mathematical calculus, Robert Boyle who introduced his famous law of atmospheric pressure, and Halley, the great astronomer, who discovered the comet named after him.

Europe was undergoing scientific revolution; political revolution was soon to follow.

2 THE FRENCH REVOLUTION

Although France was the richest and most powerful country in Europe, its peoples were badly divided and unable to cope with increasing economic and social pressures. Louis XVI, who came to the throne in 1774, was a weak and ineffective king. By going to the aid of the American colonists in their war with Britain, he ruined his country's finances. In order to obtain money, he tried to raise a tax on land which everybody, including the aristocracy, would have to pay. Opposition was so determined that the King dropped the idea, but not before he had alienated many of the nobles. Next, he attempted to get the *parlement* of Paris, a court of law, to pass new taxes. The *parlement* refused and denounced the King as a tyrant. Neither could Louis expect support from the peasants; most of them lived in terrible poverty, and hated the King, the aristocracy and the bourgeoisie alike.

A portrait of Louis XVI of France. His donations to the cause of the American colonists crippled the French economy.

As Turgot, Louis XVI's chief minister, stated, 'The nation is a society composed of different orders, badly united, and of a people whose members have so few ties with each other that in consequence everyone is concerned merely with his own particular interest.'

The storming of the Bastille

In 1788, Louis called the States General, a parliament representing the three estates: the aristocracy, the clergy and the bourgeoisie. This body had not met since 1614. When it became obvious that the Third Estate, the representatives of the ordinary people, were going to prove difficult, the King tried to close the building. The representatives formed the National Assembly and moved to a nearby tennis court where they took an oath not to separate until the King granted France a constitution.

When the news reached Paris, the people rioted; the French Revolution had begun. Extremists, like Camille Desmoulins, called for the immediate destruction of the old regime. On 14 July 1789, a mob of Parisians forced its way into the Bastille, a great prison and symbol of royal power, and released the inmates. The mob armed itself with the weapons that were kept there and defied the King's mercenary soldiers who had been sent to overawe them.

Faced by riots, the King gave way and recognized the revolutionary

The storming of the Bastille on 14 July 1789 marked the beginning of the French Revolution.

government, or Commune of Paris. A National Guard, or militia, was created. The National Assembly abolished the special rights of the aristocracy and clergy and published a Declaration of Rights. Encouraged by these successes, a mob of women, followed by the National Guard, trudged to the royal palace of Versailles and demanded that the King return with them to Paris. Louis XVI was forced to agree and found himself at the mercy of the mob. Camille Desmoulins was triumphant: 'The King is in the Louvre [a royal palace in Paris]. The National Assembly is at the Tuileries [another palace] . . . traitors are fleeing, the clergy is humbled, the aristocracy is expiring . . . The Constitution is signed.'

The fate of Louis XVI

In despair, Louis tried to escape from France in June 1791. He intended to place himself at the head of a foreign army so that he could destroy his enemies. However, he was captured at Varennes and returned to Paris where he was stripped of his remaining powers. A new Legislative Assembly was set up, but the real power lay with the extremists of the Jacobin Club who demanded that France become a republic. Another extreme group, called the Girondists, insisted that France should declare war on its enemies in Europe before they could attack her. The Girondists had their way: in April 1792, France declared war on Austria.

The cost of the war forced the government to raise taxes and prices leapt up. The French people were furious. Worse still, the Austrian commander declared that he intended to restore Louis XVI's powers.

By 1791, power in France was in the hands of the extremist members of the Jacobin Club.

Following his attempted escape and recapture, Louis XVI's fate was never really in doubt, and he was guillotined on 21 January 1793.

The King believed that he was saved and wrote: 'I must act as though I were supporting the war freely. . . . My conduct must be such that in misfortune the nation will see its own salvation in throwing itself into my arms.' On 10 August 1792, however, the Paris mob drove the royal family from the royal palace of the Tuileries. Robespierre, a Jacobin, persuaded the Legislative Assembly to dissolve itself and issue writs for a new election. In the meantime, the King was deposed and the September Massacres took place: in four days, 1,200 royalists were murdered.

The new assembly, the National Convention, tried the King, found him guilty of conspiring with the enemies of France, and sent him to the guillotine. According to a royalist, his death on 21 January 1793 'spread dismay everywhere and even the most ardent supporters of the revolution found the measure both excessive and dangerous.'

A young noble and his family are led in to suffer the summary justice of a revolutionary tribunal during the Terror.

Robespierre and the Terror

A twelve-man Committee of Public Safety was set up and, with Robespierre effectively at its head, ruled the whole of France for a time. Obsessed with the idea of a foreign plot, and convinced that he was surrounded by spies and plotters, Robespierre came to regard anyone who disagreed with him as a traitor. He set out to destroy those who opposed him, and in the Reign of Terror he masterminded, 2,600 men and women were guillotined.

Robespierre was a great idealist as well as one of the most ruthless of the extremists. He wrote: 'We desire an order in which all base and cruel feelings are suppressed by laws, and all kindly and generous feelings fostered.' The Terror was his means of achieving this 'order'.

Eventually, however, Robespierre was destroyed by his own weapon. No one's life was safe as long as he remained in power; he was too dangerous to be allowed to live. On 27 July 1794 he was denounced

Execution de Robespierre et de ses Complices Conspirateurs contre la Liberté et L'Egalité.

1 Cidevant garde Meubles	8 Le traitre Robespierre le jeune.
2 Entrée du cidevant Jardin des Thuileries a la place de la Revolution.	9 Hanriot ex Commandant de la Garde Nationale parisienne.
3 Le faubourg St Germain.	10 Le Tyran Robespierre l'ainé.
4 Sanson l'executeur de Paris.	11 Dumas ex président du Tribunale Revolutionnaire.
5 Le traitre Labas qui s'est brulé la Cervelle.	12 Le Scelerat Saint Just.
6 Le traitre Couthon deja éxécuté.	13 Lescot Fleuriot ex Maire de Paris.
7 La tête du dit Scelerat.	14 Les 14. autres Complices aussi sur 2. Charretes

L'execution a eu lieu le 10. Thermidor l'an = *de la Republique française une et indivisible.*

A contemporary illustration of the death of Robespierre and his allies. The heading reads: 'Long live the National Convention which by its energy and watchfulness has delivered the Republic from its tyrants.'

before the Convention, arrested, and sent to the guillotine the following day. With his death, the Reign of Terror came to an end. The French had defeated their European enemies and could afford to relax. As a result, the Convention set up the Directory, which became the government of France. They decided: 'To wage war on royalism, to revive patriotism, to suppress factions, to establish harmony, to restore peace, to regenerate morals, to revive commerce and industry, to awaken the arts and sciences, to restore social order, in a word, to give the French Republic the happiness and glory which it wants.'

The rise of Napoleon

The brief rule of the Directory saw the rise to prominence of Napoleon Bonaparte, a brilliant Corsican soldier. However, the success of the Revolutionary armies frightened the other European Powers. Austria, Prussia, Britain, Spain, Holland and Piedmont formed a coalition. At first, the Coalition was successful, but the French hit back in 1795.

The Austrian Netherlands were captured and French armies reached the Rhine. Holland was defeated and became an independent republic. Prussia and Spain made peace. Napoleon led his army into Italy and thrashed the Austrians at the Battle of Rivoli. Austria made peace. Only Britain continued to defy Revolutionary France. In 1798, Napoleon set out for Egypt to break Britain's control of the Mediterranean and extend French influence in the Near East. The great general's victories were nullified, however, when Horatio Nelson and the Royal Navy destroyed his fleet at the Battle of Aboukir Bay.

Meanwhile, Britain, Russia, Austria, Sicily and Portugal had formed the Second Coalition, and everywhere, French armies came under heavy pressure. The inefficiency of the Directory led to increasing discontent in France. In these circumstances, Napoleon deserted his army in Egypt, returned to France and overthrew the Directory. A new executive, the Consulate, was set up with Napoleon as First Consul. The French Revolution was over, but its ideals of Liberty, Fraternity and Equality were spreading throughout Europe. Things were never to be quite the same again.

The young Napoleon Bonaparte returned to Paris from Egypt, overthrew the Directory, and brought the French Revolution to an end.

3 NAPOLEON

On becoming First Consul, Napoleon entered into a brilliant phase of his career. In June 1800 he defeated the Austrians at Marengo in Italy. The Second Coalition collapsed and once again Britain found herself isolated. In 1802, France and Britain made peace by the Treaty of Amiens. The Revolutionary Wars were over. Within twelve months, however, the Napoleonic Wars had started and were to last from 1803 to 1815.

Once again the all-conquering French armies were on the march, and Napoleon was determined to destroy Britain, his most stubborn enemy. A great force was drawn up on the Channel coast facing England, while the French fleet tricked Nelson into thinking it was about to attack the West Indies. However, realizing his mistake, Nelson chased the French flotilla back across the Atlantic to Spain and destroyed it at the Battle of Trafalgar in October 1805.

Nelson's defeat of the combined French and Spanish fleet at Trafalgar finally put paid to Napoleon's plan to invade Britain.

Emperor of the French

Elsewhere, however, Napoleon was unbeatable. His secretary, de Bourienne, wrote, 'Were I to attempt to describe the brilliant campaign of 1805, I must set down a victory every day. ... On the 24th of September he [Napoleon] left Paris, hostilities commenced on the 2nd October, on the 6th and 7th the French had passed the Danube and turned the enemy's army. On the 8th Murat [one of Napoleon's generals] at the battle of Wertigen upon the Danube made 2,000 Austrians prisoner ... our victorious legions entered on the 10th into Augsburg and on the 12th into Munich.' Austria made peace shortly afterwards.

Napoleon crushed the Prussians at Jena in 1806 and the Russians at Friedland in 1807. New kingdoms were created to be ruled by Napoleon's brothers: Louis received Holland, Joseph Naples and Jerome

Murat leads the French cavalry to victory over the Prussians at the Battle of Jena in 1806.

Following his conquests, Napoleon created new kingdoms to be ruled over by his brothers. This is Joseph, King of Naples.

Westphalia. The Holy Roman Empire was dissolved. In his memoirs, Napoleon declared: 'One of my great plans was the reforming of the concentration of those same geographical nations which have been disunited and parcelled out by revolution and policy'. However, it is much more likely that he intended to create a huge French empire surrounded by smaller satellite states. Even before he achieved his greatest military successes, Napoleon made himself Emperor of the French in 1804. He swept aside the romantic notions of the revolution: 'France', he said, 'needs no constitution; it is essentially a monarchical country. To have an assembly is a sure way to start a revolution. It immediately splits the nation into two parties, with the resulting feuds and passions.' Although Napoleon despised representative government, he fully appreciated the importance of an efficient administration and local government. He divided France up into *départements* (provinces), *arrondissements* (districts) and *communes* (towns) ruled by government officials. The old social order was ignored and promotion by merit became the order of the day.

This cartoon shows Napoleon driving out the forces of equality. He was no believer in representative government.

The restrictions on trade were abolished. The Bank of France was founded and stabilized the French economy. French law was simplified and organized as the *Code Napoléon*. Something like a state education system was created: the Church and municipal authorities provided primary schools, while the state provided 100 secondary schools, 45 special *lycées* for highly intelligent pupils, and the Imperial University. Napoleon established good relations with the Church by the Concordat of 1802, in which he recognized Roman Catholicism as the established faith and agreed to pay the salaries of bishops and clergy. The revolutionary ideal of equality was ignored. Napoleon's brothers were made kings and his greatest generals became princes and dukes.

To a certain extent, Napoleonic France was a police state. The news-sheets were carefully censored so that the general public only heard what the government wanted them to know. Many people who opposed the regime were imprisoned and a few, like the royalist Duke of Enghien, were murdered. People were encouraged to denounce the disloyal and there were many government spies. Although the Napoleonic government frequently interfered in the lives of its people, it was much more efficient than its predecessors.

While Napoleon was reorganizing France, his military conquests continued. He decided to bring Britain to her knees by forbidding all the countries under French influence to trade with her—the so-called Continental System. When Portugal ignored his instructions, Napoleon ordered an army to occupy Portugal and Spain. To counter this move, Britain sent an expeditionary force to Portugal and the Peninsular War (1808–14) started. General Wellesley, the future Duke of Wellington, gradually pushed back the French armies with the help of Portuguese and Spanish guerrillas.

Decline and fall

Napoleon's luck had changed. In 1811, Tsar Alexander of Russia broke away from the Continental System, and Napoleon collected an enormous army of 600,000 men and invaded Russia. Although Napoleon won a number of battles and occupied Moscow, the Russian capital, his campaign failed. The retreat from Moscow, which took place during one of the bitterest winters on record, reduced the French army to 30,000 men. One observer recalled: 'the poor wretches [the soldiers] dragged themselves along, shivering, with chattering teeth, until the snow packed under the soles of their boots, a bit of debris, or the body of a fallen comrade tripped them and threw them down. Then their moans for help went unheeded. The snow soon covered them

Beginning in October 1812, the retreat from Moscow decimated the once mighty French army.

up and only low white mounds showed where they lay. Our road was strewn with these hummocks like a cemetery.'

The enemies of France sensed Napoleon's weakness and formed the Fourth Coalition in 1813. Napoleon was defeated at Leipzig, and Italy and the Netherlands were lost. By the spring of 1814, France's enemies had reached her frontiers and Napoleon accepted the Peace of Paris. The Emperor abdicated and was exiled to Elba. However, while the

Wellington urges his men on to victory during the Battle of Waterloo in June 1815.

allies were preparing to redraw the maps of Europe at the Congress of Vienna, it was announced that 'the monster is loose.'

Napoleon had escaped from Elba and in March 1815 re-entered France, where many of his old generals and soldiers joined him. Strong armies under the Duke of Wellington and Marshal Blucher of Prussia met Napoleon at the Battle of Waterloo. Captain John Pringle described the turning point in the struggle: 'The [British] men fired independently, retiring a few paces to load, and then advanced and fired, so that their fire never ceased for a moment. The French ... still advanced, notwithstanding the severe loss they sustained. ... They were now within about fifty yards of our line. ... They could not, however, deploy under such fire; and from that moment they ceased to advance, their chance of success over.'

Once again, Napoleon had to abdicate and was exiled to the lonely islet of St Helena in the middle of the South Atlantic Ocean. Here, he died a disappointed man in 1821. Napoleon summed up his achievements in this way: 'A man is only a man. His power is nothing if circumstances are not favourable. Opinion is all important. If I had not appeared someone else would have done the same thing. I consider that I count for no more than half in the battles which I have won. The general's name is hardly worth mentioning, for the fact is that it is the army which wins the battle.'

At its greatest extent, Napoleon's empire covered most of Europe from Spain to the borders of Russia and the Ottoman Empire.

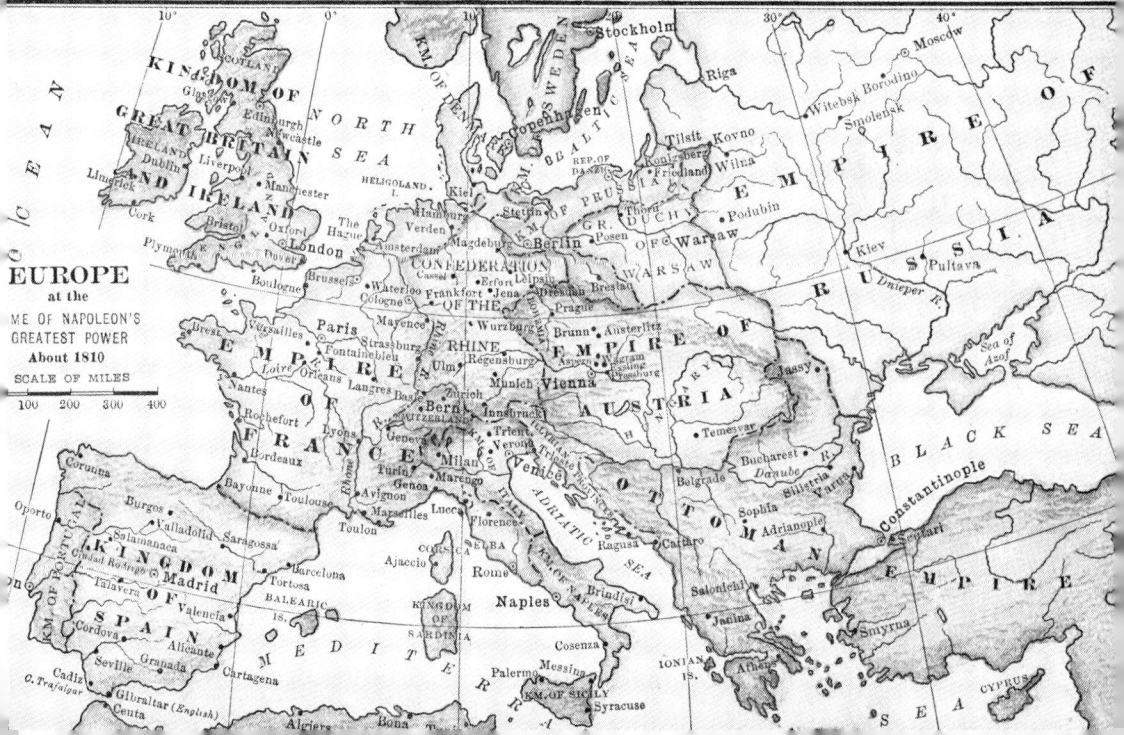

4 THE AGRICULTURAL REVOLUTION

Although the farmers of Europe were some of its most conservative inhabitants, changes in farming methods, new crops and new machinery were introduced during the period from 1650 to 1850.

Townshend and Bakewell

During the Middle Ages, most livestock had to be slaughtered in the autumn due to lack of winter feed. In the seventeenth century, East Anglian farmers started growing various root crops with which to feed their animals during the winter. However, it took over a century to convince most farmers that root crops were the answer to their problem. Viscount Townshend (1674–1738) clearly demonstrated their effectiveness on his estates in Norfolk, and as a result became known as 'Turnip' Townshend.

In this painting, a farmer is preparing a root crop to be used as feed for an improbably large ox.

Eighteenth-century cattle and sheep were much smaller than modern breeds. Robert Bakewell (1725–95) of Dishley in Leicestershire introduced selective breeding: only the best bulls and rams were allowed to mate with the females of their species. As a result, the average weight and quality of cattle and sheep improved steadily throughout the period. In 1750, 71,000 cattle and 656,000 sheep were sold at Smithfield Market; in 1800, 125,000 cattle and 842,000 sheep were sold; and in 1850, 227,000 cattle and 1,540,000 sheep. Gradually, meat became a normal part of the working man's diet and not a luxury for the well-to-do.

Selective and cross breeding brought about similar improvements in cereal production and, for a time, Britain became an exporter of corn. Better land utilization was made possible by the development of more sophisticated crop rotations, like the famous Four-Year Norfolk System, consisting of annual crops of turnips, barley, clover and wheat. These new methods enabled farmers to grow crops on all their land every year without reducing yields. The nitrates the cereal crops absorbed from the soil were replaced by leguminous crops, such as clover, which contained bacteria in their roots which fixed the nitrogen of the air.

Robert Bakewell's selective breeding methods helped farmers to increase the weight and quality of their animals.

Jethro Tull's horse-drawn seed drill made sowing much quicker and less labour intensive, much to the dismay of agricultural labourers.

Enclosures

Enclosures were a third way of improving land utilization. During the Middle Ages, most peasants were given a selection of strips in each of their village's great 'open fields'. However, most farmers came to believe that smaller, consolidated fields could be cultivated more efficiently than strips. As a result, the open fields were divided into a number of compact fields surrounded by hedges. Many enclosures took place by common consent; even more were accomplished by Act of Parliament. An Enclosure Commissioner lamented that he had been 'accessory to the injuring of 2,000 poor people at the rate of 20 families per parish.' Arthur Young, an agricultural expert, claimed that 'By nineteen out of twenty Enclosure Bills the poor are injured and some grossly injured.' Occasionally, enclosures were forced on the poor. Although they often rioted and smashed down the new hedges, in the end the poor had no alternative but to accept the situation and become landless labourers.

These changes brought about a revolution in the nature of rural society. Instead of the old order of lords of the manor, yeomen and peasant farmers, the country world was made up of landowners, tenant farmers and landless labourers.

The new large farms provided marvellous opportunities for the use of agricultural machinery. Jethro Tull (1674–1740) introduced a horse drawn mechanical seed drill. Later, in the nineteenth century, mechanical reapers and threshers were introduced. These new machines were unpopular with the labourers as they reduced the need for workers.

Captain Swing

The workers' anger led to the 'Last Labourers' Revolt' in 1830. Rioting, rick burning and machinery smashing started in Kent and spread to Sussex, Hampshire, Surrey and many other counties. Farmers even received threatening letters signed by 'Captain Swing'. The Duke of

During the Last Labourers' Revolt, many magistrates were forced to accede to the demands of the rioters.

WE the undersigned Magistrates acting in and for the Hundred of Gallow, in the County of Norfolk, do promise to use our utmost Endeavours and Influence we may possess, to prevail upon the Occupiers of Land in the said Hundred,

To discontinue the use of Thrashing Machines, and to take them to pieces.

Dated this 29th. day of November, 1830.

CHAS. TOWNSHEND.
ROBERT NORRIS.
EDW. MARSHAM.

Buckingham wrote 'this part of the country [Hampshire] is wholly in the hands of the rebels. 1,500 rioters are to assemble tomorrow morning and will attack any farmhouses where there are threshing machines. They go about levying contributions on every gentleman's house. There are very few magistrates and what there are are completely cowed.' There was no revolution, however. Shows of military force and a large number of arrests ended the disorders. Ninety special courts in 34 counties tried nearly 2,000 peasants, 19 of whom were hanged, 481 transported (sent to prisons in the colonies) and 664 imprisoned.

In spite of these disorders, more and more farmers adopted the new methods, crops and machinery. One of the main reasons for this was the work of propagandists like Arthur Young (1741–1820), who between 1784 and 1809 edited the *Annals of Agriculture*. Another expert, William Marshall (1745–1818), published *A Survey of Rural Economy* in 1787, in which he pointed out that owners had to analyse their farms before they could improve them. He described his own methods in this way: 'I have studied the map of this noble farm, traced its outlines, and examined repeatedly every field and parcel of it. ... I have registered the arrangement, tabled the crops and fallows ... I have drawn up a table of livestock ... the quantity of manure, the implements, etc.'

Following the example of Thomas Coke, other landowners invited farmers to sheep-shearing meetings and demonstrated the improvements they had made to their estates. The picture shows one such meeting in progress at Woburn, the home of the Duke of Bedford.

A playing card showing a workhouse scene.

Thomas Coke (1752–1842) of Holkham in Norfolk also played an important part in spreading the new ideas. When he took over his estates in 1776, they were worth £2,200 a year in rents. As a result of the improvements he carried out they yielded £20,000 in rents in

1816. Every year, Coke held a sheep-shearing meeting which was attended by farmers from all over the country who came to see what 'modern' farming methods were like.

The rural poor

These changes greatly increased crop production, providing food for the rapidly growing populations of the industrial towns. However, the rural population was also increasing, despite large-scale migration to the towns, and this led to serious underemployment in the countryside. In 1795, the Berkshire magistrates decided to subsidize the labourers' wages out of the Poor Rates when the price of bread rose. 'Everybody must have observed', wrote D. Davies in 1787, 'that families with four or five young children are common in country parishes. As bread makes the principal part of the food of all poor families ... it is manifest that whatever causes operate in raising at any time the price of corn, the same necessarily bring heavy distress upon the families of this description.'

In some counties, the magistrates adopted the 'Roundsman' system: well-to-do farmers employed paupers on reduced wages with the difference being provided by the Poor Rate. In other places, the poor were provided with allotments. Unfortunately, Edwin Chadwick, one of the great social reformers of the first half of the nineteenth century, believed that these methods were making labourers into mindless paupers. The Poor Law Amendment Act of 1834 incorporated many of his ideas, and people who could not support themselves were ordered to be sent to workhouses. Conditions in these 'Bastilles' were made deliberately unpleasant. For, as the Poor Law Commissioners put it: 'Every penny bestowed that tends to render the condition of the pauper more eligible than that of the independent labourer is a bounty on indolence and vice.' Riots greeted the introduction of workhouses, and an Anti-Poor Law League was set up.

Conditions were far worse on the Continent. In France before the Revolution, land belonged to the Crown, Church, nobility and wealthy townspeople. Most tenant farmers handed over half their produce as rent. Large landowners also dominated agriculture in eastern Europe and Russia. However, interest in agricultural improvements became widespread after 1750. In Austria, Prussia, Denmark and Savoy considerable progress was made towards the abolition of serfdom.

Reform came slowly, however. In 1852, a Frenchman wrote, 'A thirteenth-century peasant would visit many of our farms without much astonishment.' Real change did not come until after 1850 when the opening of the railway system encouraged commercial farming. Soon, however, the European farmer was fighting to survive the competition of his rivals in the New World and Australia.

5 THE INDUSTRIAL REVOLUTION

The rates of invention and industrial progress in Britain between 1750 and 1850 were revolutionary. This was not true, however, of Europe as a whole. In 1800, Britain produced 10 million tonnes of coal while Germany, France and Belgium only raised 6 million tonnes between them. Bar iron cost about £10 a tonne in Britain in 1825 and £26 a tonne in France. In most aspects of technological change, Britain led the way and soon became the 'workshop of the world'.

The power of steam
The provision of new sources of power was the inspiration for many changes. Although the steam engine had been introduced towards the end of the seventeenth century, it did not really have a significant effect until James Watt invented the separate condenser which greatly increased its efficiency. Watt's use of the sun-and-planets gear to

James Watt greatly improved the power, efficiency and versatility of the steam engine.

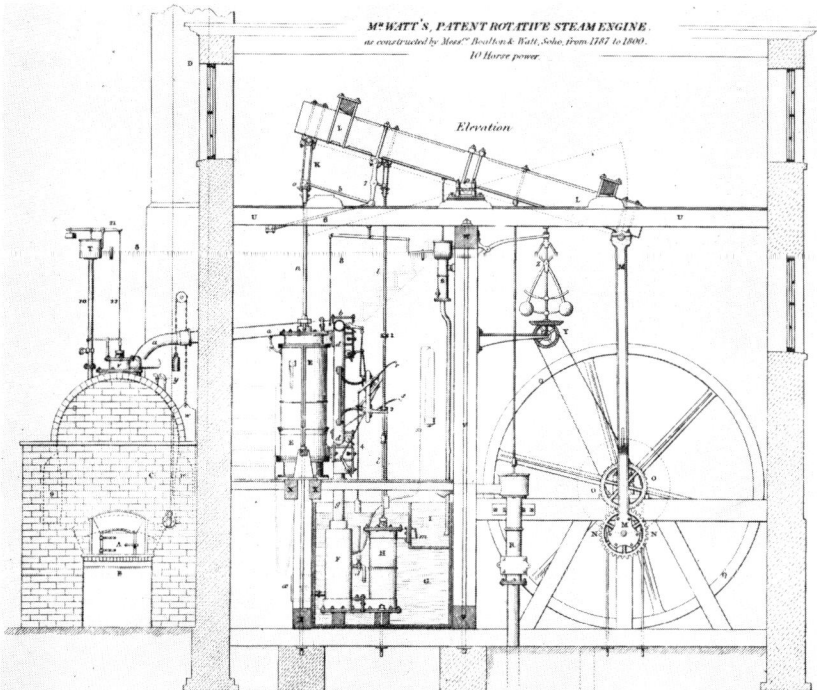

MR WATT'S, PATENT ROTATIVE STEAM ENGINE.
as constructed by Messrs Boulton & Watt, Soho, from 1787 to 1800.
10 Horse power.

Elevation

convert the engine's backwards and forwards movement into rotary motion enabled the machines to be used for a much wider variety of purposes. They were used to pump water out of coal mines, operate bellows in blast furnaces and maintain water levels in canals. Thomas Young wrote, 'These steam engines are said to save three-fourths of the fuel formerly used. ... Such a machine performs the work of 120 horses working 8 hours each day. ... The steam engine [has] been brought very near to perfection by the improvements of Mr Watt.'

The invention of an efficient steam engine made possible a great increase in coal production. Miners were able to excavate deeper seams as they were able to pump out the water which collected in the tunnels. Ventilation was provided by installing 'up' and 'down' shafts with a furnace at the bottom of the 'up' shaft. The furnace heated the air

In this illustration of 1814, one steam engine raises coal from the mine while another powers a train carrying the coal to a nearby town.

above it so that it rose and fresh air was pulled down the 'down' shaft to take its place. The fresh air was directed by 'traps' or doors. Boys of 7 or 8 years old opened and closed these traps for 6d (2½p) a day. Women hauled carts loaded with coal along the tunnels by pulling on chains which were attached to belts around their waists. As a result of these 'improvements', Britain's coal production was raised to well over 20 million tonnes a year by 1830.

Iron and steel
For many hundreds of years, iron ore had been smelted with charcoal. The heat of a charcoal fire melted, or reduced, the iron and caused some of the carbon in it to combine with the oxygen of the air to form carbon dioxide. Abraham Darby (1677–1717) discovered how to use coal as a reducing agent. As his daughter-in-law recalled: 'He first tried [to reduce iron ore] with raw coal as it came out of the mines but it did not answer. He, not discouraged, had the coal coked into cinder, as is done for drying malt, and it then succeeded to his satisfaction.' The Darbys tried to keep the knowledge of the new process a secret but their rivals gradually came to hear of it and use the idea themselves.

Unfortunately, molten iron picked up impurities from the coke, so that it could not be made into wrought iron until Henry Cort (1740–1800) invented the 'reverbatory furnace'. Inside one of these new furnaces, the pig iron was stirred or 'puddled' until its impurities combined with the oxygen of the air. As a result of Darby's and Cort's inventions, the price of iron fell dramatically from £18 a tonne in 1750 to £8 a tonne in 1820. Fine instruments, however, were made of steel, which could only be produced in small quantities until Benjamin Huntsman (1704–76) discovered that he could manufacture it by placing crucibles containing wrought iron in a furnace and introducing carbon in carefully controlled quantities.

Increasing availability of iron and steel stimulated engineers to greater efforts. Henry Maudsley invented a lathe for cutting the thread on bolts and screws, and a slide rest for guiding cutting tools on the lathe. As a result of these and other inventions by men like Joseph Whitworth, machine tools were made which produced goods to exact sizes. As soon as standardization was accomplished, spare parts could be manufactured with which to repair damaged machines. In consequence, machine manufacturing became completely reliable for the first time.

Specialization followed. Certain towns became famous for particular products. At the beginning of the nineteenth century, William Cobbett described this process: 'From this one town [Sheffield] and its environs go nine-tenths of the knives that are used in the whole world; there

During the nineteenth century, the town of Sheffield came to specialize in the manufacture of knives.

being, I understand, no knives made at Birmingham, the manufacture of which place consists of the larger sort of implements, of locks of all sorts, and guns and swords, and of all the endless articles of hardware which go to furnishing a house.'

Textiles

Since the early Middle Ages, Britain had been famous for its woollen cloth. In the eighteenth century, cloth made from cotton became popular. However, both spinning and weaving processes were slow. Weaving was revolutionized by John Kay's invention of the 'flying shuttle' in 1733. In consequence, workers using spinning wheels had difficulty keeping up with the demand for yarn. Then, in 1769, James Hargreaves invented the 'spinning jenny' which produced several threads at the same time while Richard Arkwright's 'water frame' was a power-driven spinning machine. Samuel Crompton combined the merits of the jenny and frame in his 'mule' in 1779. As a result, it was the weaving industry that could not cope with the flood of yarn until Edmund Cartwright invented the power loom in 1785.

It has been said that machines demand factories as they are expensive and require large quantities of raw materials and wide markets for their products. However, the cottage craftsmen were slow to give up their freedom. The weavers, for example, fought hard to remain independent. In 1800, there were 170,000 independent handloom weavers as against 80,000 textile factory workers. But by 1850, there were 330,000 factory workers and only 45,000 independent weavers. Factory manufacture gradually destroyed the domestic weaving industry.

Richard Arkwright's water frame was one of a number of developments which revolutionized cotton spinning.

Domestic workers reacted violently when they realized their freedom was threatened. Between 1811 and 1816, there was a series of Luddite riots. Samuel Bamford described an attack on a mill in Middleton in 1816: 'The mob halted in front of the building, and a score or two of boys who led the mob set up a shout, and began to throw stones and break the windows. A number of discharges [shots] from the mill followed ... several were wounded, and three fell dead, on seeing which the mob fled in all directions.'

The supposed leader of the Luddites rallies his men, while in the background a mill burns.

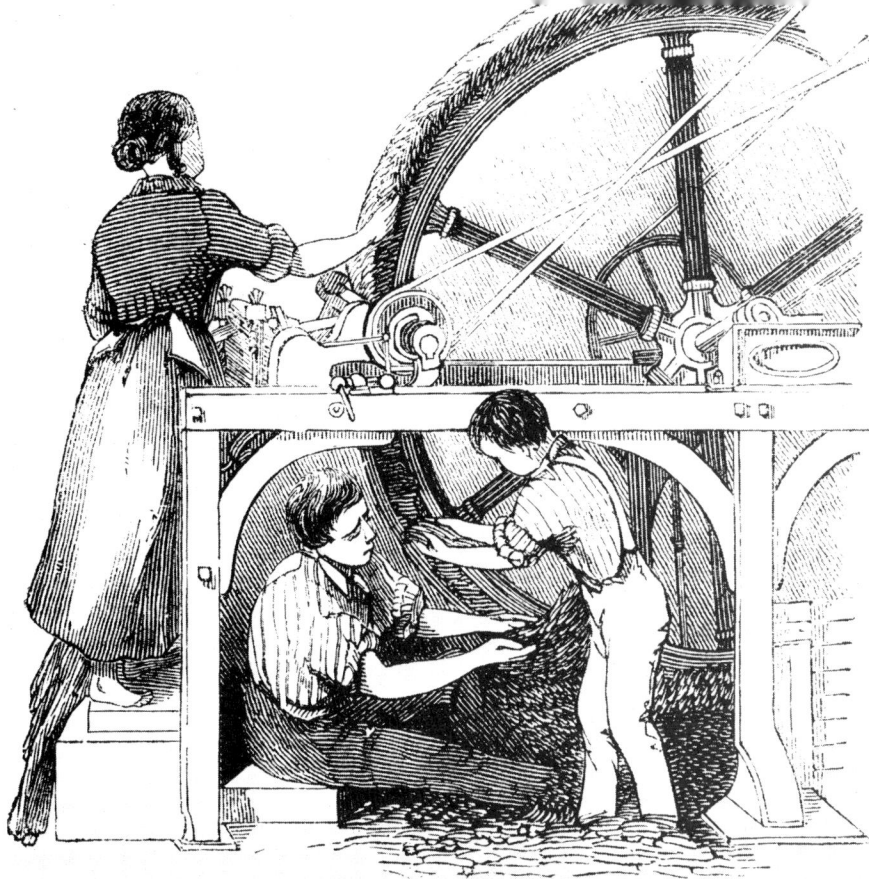

A man, a woman and a small boy working a machine used for combing wool. Conditions are cramped, and the machinery is unguarded.

Factory conditions

The factories concentrated in the towns of the Midlands and the North. Conditions were often appalling: 'In the cotton spinning work,' wrote William Cobbett, 'these creatures [the workers] are kept, fourteen hours each day, locked up, summer and winter in a heat of from eighty to eighty-four degrees . . . children are rendered decrepit and deformed by consumption [tuberculosis] before they arrive at the age of sixteen.'

Cheap buildings were erected to house the flood of country people entering the towns in search of better paid work. A French visitor to Manchester felt that 'little attention is paid to the health and convenience of the inhabitants' and commented on 'the want of public squares, fountains, trees'. According to another writer, 'The potatoes purchased by the workers are generally bad, the vegetables shrivelled, the cheese stale and of poor quality, the bacon rancid. The meat is lean, old, tough and partially tainted.'

Although conditions in most manufacturing towns were bad, there were exceptions. Josiah Wedgwood (1730–95), the great china manufacturer, was able to boast about his workers at Etruria in Staffordshire: 'The workmen earning near double their former wages—their homes mostly new and comfortable, and the lands, roads, and every other circumstance bearing evident marks of the most pleasing and rapid improvements.'

The appalling conditions existing in most areas led to a wave of reforms in the 1830s and 1840s. Factory and Mines Acts prohibited the employment of children and gradually reduced the hours of work for youths, women and adult men. This was a slow process and a number of industries remained relatively unreformed until the beginning of the twentieth century.

Josiah Wedgwood's Etruria pottery works seen from the canal built to transport goods from the factory.

6 THE TRANSPORT REVOLUTION

At the beginning of the eighteenth century, European road communications and road transport were, on the whole, inferior to those of the Romans. The roads themselves were totally unsatisfactory. Daniel Defoe, the author of *Robinson Crusoe*, noted that the London to Ipswich road was 'in time of floods dangerous, and at other times, in winter, scarce passable.' As a result 'turnpike trusts' were set up to improve stretches of particularly important highway. Turnpike Surveyors and Commissioners collected tolls from travellers using the improved roads, or 'turnpikes', and spent the money entirely upon their maintenance and improvement. By the end of the eighteenth

This engraving shows a turnpike at Hyde Park Corner in 1792.
Travellers paid their tolls in the buildings on either side of the road.

Thomas Telford's suspension bridge over the Menai Straits, built between 1820 and 1826.

century, there were over 1,000 turnpike trusts in England. Defoe thoroughly approved, arguing that 'the benefit of a good road abundantly [makes] amends for that little charge the travellers are put to at the turnpikes.'

The road-builders

New approaches to road-making developed. Blind John Metcalf of Knaresborough (1717–1810) cambered his roads to improve their drainage. Thomas Telford (1757–1834) built 920 miles of road and over 1,000 bridges including the magnificent suspension bridge across the Menai Straits between North Wales and Anglesey. Telford constructed his roads on expensive stone foundations, but John MacAdam (1756–1836) argued that such foundations were unnecessary if the road surface was good enough. He developed a waterproof covering made of small crushed stones mixed with fine dust and water to produce a kind of cement. MacAdam's technique was, at £88 a mile, much cheaper than Telford's which cost £105 a mile.

These improvements considerably shortened travel times. In 1715 it took 8 days to travel from London to York; by 1830 the journey only took 3 days. An observer pointed out in 1768: 'Posting is much more easy, convenient and reasonable upon a just comparison of all circumstances, in England, than in France. The English carriages, horses, harness, and roads are better.' Nevertheless, stage coach journeys were usually very uncomfortable. William Cobbett recalled, 'To travel in stage coaches was to be hurried along by force, in a box, with an air hole in it, and constantly exposed to broken limbs.'

Waterways

The cheapest way of moving heavy goods was by sail on river or sea. Since before Tudor times, the transportation of coal to London had been entirely by sea. Groceries of all sorts were sent out by water from London, Bristol and Liverpool, as were tanned hides, corn, slates, iron ore, timber, and tobacco.

A view of the Bridgwater Canal and Worsley Hall, the home of the Duke of Bridgwater.

Although means of maintaining constant levels of water, like the pound lock and sluice gates, were well known at the beginning of the eighteenth century, the Canal Age did not really get under way until the 1760s. The Duke of Bridgwater took the lead by constructing a superb waterway from his mines at Worsley to Manchester between 1759 and 1761. The Duke employed a great engineer called James Brindley (1716–72) to supervise the work. Brindley tried to maintain the level of his canals without the use of locks. Whenever faced by a difficult problem, 'he usually went to bed and lay there working it out in his head till the design was complete.' The canal cut the cost of coal in Manchester from 11s 8d (58p) to 2s 6d (12½p) a tonne. A nationwide network of canals was constructed linking Britain's rivers and coastlines.

Canal travel was slow but pleasant, and many people journeyed by stage boat: 'The shape of the machine resembles the common representations of Noah's ark. . . . Within this floating house are two apartments, seats in which are hired at different prices, the parlour and the kitchen. Two horses, harnessed one before the other, tow it along at the rate of a league (about 3 miles) an hour.'

The Railway Age

A rival to the canals appeared in the 1830s. As a contemporary predicted, 'Excellent as these canals are, railroads are found to accomplish the same purpose at less expense. In these the wheels of the carriage move in grooves upon iron bars laid all along the road.' By 1820, more than 1,500 miles of 'tramways' had been built along which carriages could be hauled or pushed. Inventors were already trying to produce an efficient locomotive. A Frenchman named Cugnot was the first to succeed, in 1769. In the years that followed, William Murdock, Richard Trevithick, William Hedley and George Stephenson gradually improved upon his design. The most famous early locomotive was Stephenson's *Rocket.* According to the poet Southey, 'She consisted of a boiler, a stove, a small platform, a bench, and behind the bench a barrel, containing enough water to prevent her being thirsty for fifteen miles. . . . She goes upon ten wheels which are her feet, and are moved by bright steel legs called pistons; these are propelled by steam. . . . Mr Stephenson, having taken me on the bench of the engine with him, we started at about ten miles an hour.'

The opening of the Stockton–Darlington Railway in 1825 was the beginning of the Railway Age. By the 1830s and 40s Britain was in the grip of 'railway mania', and lines were built in all directions. In 1835, 340 miles of track carried 4 million passengers. By 1855, 7,300 miles of track carried 111.4 million passengers. Railway development affected most aspects of life. For instance, as people could live quite

A sketch showing the opening of the Stockton-Darlington Railway on 27 September 1825.

long distances away from their place of work, dormitory towns like Surbiton in Surrey grew up. Market gardens and dairy farms deep in the country could rush their produce to the towns. Goods and passengers could be conveyed rapidly all over the land.

From clippers to steamships
Shipping experienced a similar transformation. The Americans brought about a breakthrough in sailing ship design by introducing 'clipper'

ships in 1845. These long, narrow, sharp-prowed ships cut their way through the water while their deep keels provided greater stability. Clippers could reach speeds of fifteen knots (about 17 m.p.h.), and rival ships raced each other to and from India and Australia.

In 1736, Jonathan Hull managed to adapt a Newcomen steam engine to operate paddles in a barge, and so produced the first of a series of experimental steamships. The first successful British steamer was William Symington's *Charlotte Dundas* of 1801. Other inventors succeeded in producing iron ships. John Laird launched Britain's first at Birkenhead in 1829. The *Sirius* iron ship steamed from London to New York in 16½ days in 1838. A few hours later, Isambard Kingdom Brunel's *Great Western* anchored near her, having steamed from Bristol to New York in 14 days.

These advances in shipbuilding enabled Britain to dominate the world. The Royal Navy was more powerful than all the other fleets in the world put together and the Merchant Marine took British goods

Rival clipper ships raced each other to bring back their cargoes from Asia and Australia in the shortest time.

Isambard Kingdom Brunel's steamship the Great Western *arrives in New York after her first voyage across the Atlantic, in 1838.*

to every corner of the earth. Vast quantities of sugar, tea and spices, wool, cotton and timber were imported; the chief export was textiles. Britain's trade continually expanded: in 1750 more than half of the country's goods were sold to Europe; in 1850, however, two-thirds were sold to non-European countries.

Similar developments took place all over Europe. After 1815, the main German rivers were improved, and steam tugs appeared on them in the 1840s. The successful development of steam traction in Britain led to the building of some railways in most European countries by 1848. Many of the lines were installed by British engineers and workers. At first the French Government was rather slow to perceive the importance of railways, but by 1850 France, too, possessed a network of main lines.

Improvements in transport affected every aspect of European life and brought its nations closer together, at least as far as travel times were concerned.

7 ROMANTICISM

Until the middle of the eighteenth century, most artists, architects, writers and composers based their work on sets of formal rules, many of them arising from the study of Graeco-Roman art. These artists belonged to what was known as the Classical Movement. During the course of the eighteenth century, most of these ideas were questioned and a new movement, called Romanticism, emerged. Romanticism was a reaction against reason, artificiality and display, and was marked by a love of the unusual and the highly emotional.

Painting
Eugene Delacroix (1798–1863), a Frenchman, was one of the great Romantic painters. He was bitterly attacked by the critics of the time for his use of brilliant colour and the exotic nature of his paintings. He took a passionate interest in horses, which he painted to perfection.

Dorchester Mead *by J. M. W. Turner.*

He visited England where he admired the superb animal paintings of George Stubbs (1724–1806) and the country scenes of William Constable (1776–1837).

Joseph Mallord William Turner (1775–1851) was probably the greatest English romantic painter. He, like Delacroix, was viciously attacked by the Classicists, who described his landscapes as 'pictures of nothing'. The magnificence of his work was finally recognized by the famous art critic John Ruskin in a book called *Modern Painters*. Ruskin insisted that Turner's work was superior to that of the ancient masters.

Architecture

In architecture, the Romantic movement caused a revival of the Gothic style. Horace Walpole led the way in Britain by building Strawberry Hill, a country mansion at Twickenham near London. Although Gothic architecture was quite popular in England, it reached much greater heights in France and Germany, and later in Italy and Russia. In Britain, the Houses of Parliament, the London Law Courts and

The British Houses of Parliament, built in the Gothic style by Charles Barry and Augustus Welby Pugin.

A portrait of the novelist and poet Sir Walter Scott, painted by Sir Edwin Landseer in 1824.

the University of Glasgow are good examples of the revived style. Other major examples were Vienna's Town Hall and the Hungarian Houses of Parliament in Budapest.

Romanticism also showed itself in eighteenth century architects' delight in the exotic. Europeans became fascinated by Chinese art. Pagodas, such as that at Kew Gardens, were built all over Europe. The love of 'Chinoiserie' affected the design of the interior of the Royal Pavilion at Brighton, the Tea House at Potsdam in Prussia, and the Palazzina at Palermo in Sicily.

Literature
In literature, the leader of the Romantic Movement was Sir Walter Scott (1771–1832). His studies of the past inspired him to write a series of exciting romances, called the Waverley novels. Among the most famous were *Ivanhoe* (1819), *Kenilworth* (1821) and *Quentin Durward* (1823). Gothic romances were also popular. Horace Walpole's *Castle of Otranto* (1776), Mrs Radcliffe's *The Mysteries of Udolpho* (1794) and Mary Shelley's *Frankenstein* (1818) provided the reading public with all the horrors and sensations it required. Of course many other kinds of novel were written: Jane Austen (1775–1817) produced a series

of brilliant social comedies including *Pride and Prejudice, Sense and Sensibility, Mansfield Park* and *Emma*, while Maria Edgeworth (1767–1849), Thomas Peacock (1785–1866) and Captain Marryat (1792–1848) also enjoyed considerable popularity. Some of Charles Dickens' finest novels were written during this period, including *Pickwick Papers* (1837), *Oliver Twist* (1839), *Nicholas Nickleby* (1839), *Martin Chuzzlewit* (1844) and *Dombey and Son* (1848).

Lord Byron led the European Romantic Movement in poetry. His poems were passionate and melodramatic. In *The Giaour*, for instance, Hassan discovers that his mistress, Leila, is in love with a young Venetian, known as the Giaour, or Infidel. In his jealous rage, he drowns Leila and is killed by the Giaour, who then enters a monastery. Curiously, Byron's poetry was much more popular abroad than in his own country. His great fame rested to a certain extent on the support he gave to subject peoples like the Greeks. 'I have simplified my politics,' he said, 'into detestation of all existing governments.'

Percy Bysshe Shelley (1792–1822) was also a revolutionary. He

The poet Lord Byron.

Percy Bysshe Shelley.

proclaimed his horror of the 'successive tyrannies in France'. Shelley wanted to see English society reformed although he declared, 'It is a mistake to suppose that I dedicate my poetical compositions solely to the direct enforcement of reform. . . . My purpose has hitherto been simply to familiarize the highly refined imagination of the more select classes of poetical readers with beautiful idealisms of moral excellence.'

Two truly great poets, William Wordsworth (1770–1854) and Samuel Taylor Coleridge (1772–1834), believed passionately in the power of nature to transform mankind. Wordsworth changed the language of poetry. In the preface to *The Lyrical Ballads*, he wrote, 'The principal object, then, proposed in these poems, was to choose incidents and situations from common life, and to relate or describe these throughout, as far as was possible, in a selection of language actually used by men.' Coleridge produced both simple and exotic poems. 'Christabel', a story of witchcraft, is of delicate beauty. In this extract, Coleridge describes how Christabel is bewitched:

A snake's small eye blinks dull and shy;
And the lady's eyes they shrink in her head.
Each shrunk up to a serpent's eye,
And with somewhat of malice, and more of dread,
At Christabel she looked askance.—
One moment and the sight was fled.
But Christabel in dizzy trance
Stumbling on the unsteady ground
Shuddered aloud, with a hissing sound.

The Romantic composers
The Romantic Revolution also affected the world of music. Hitherto, musicians, and even great composers like Haydn and Mozart, had been servants in some grand person's household. Ludwig van Beethoven (1770–1827) refused to enter anyone's service and earned his living by teaching and composing. His music suited the age: it was grand and passionate. He perfected the sonata, particularly the piano sonata, and produced a series of magnificent symphonies.

The three giants of Romantic Music were Robert Schumann (1810–56), Frederic Chopin (1810–49) and Felix Mendelssohn (1809–47). Schumann had hoped to become a great pianist, but crippled one of his hands. One summer, however, he met the German poet Heine and decided to set his poems to music. Chopin was a magical Polish pianist and composer. Although deeply distressed by the sufferings of his own people, who were Russian subjects, Chopin produced a delightful mixture of tender, dreamy music and some very rousing tunes—including preludes, nocturnes, waltzes, mazurkas, polonaises and ballades.

The great composer Ludwig van Beethoven.

Mendelssohn was born in Hamburg, Germany, but regarded Britain as his second home. 'Even in the glowing sun of Italy,' he said, 'I have thought with pleasure of your dear, smoky London, which seems to wrap itself round me like a friendly cloak.' Much of his best work was inspired by Britain. He composed intriguing incidental music for *A Midsummer Night's Dream* and wrote his oratorio *Elijah*, for the Birmingham Music Festival. In 1842, he played the piano before Queen Victoria and Prince Albert.

The Romantic composers broke away from the formalism and stiffness of the eighteenth century, and much of their music expressed the mood or feeling conveyed in an idea or poem. Franz Liszt (1811–86), a great Hungarian pianist-composer, wrote a series of fine 'Symphonic Poems,' although it was Richard Wagner (1813–83) who took the Romantic ideal furthest, in a number of great operas including *The Ring of the Nibelung*.

In the world of art, as in that of politics and technology, the Age of Revolution was a period of differing opinions and warring factions. Yet out of these struggles emerged a great deal that was beautiful and memorable.

An early daguerrotype photograph of Frederick Chopin.

8 REVOLUTION IN EUROPE, 1815–48

The French Revolution and the exploits of Bonaparte had a deep and lasting effect on the peoples of Europe. 'Within every European country,' one diplomat wrote, 'a burning fever is at work; the harbinger of the most violent convulsions which the civilized world has known since the fall of the Roman Empire.'

The 1815 Congress of Vienna redrew the boundaries of Europe, and restored most of the countries to their pre-revolutionary form. However, some of the states bordering France were strengthened so that they could help curb her ambitions: Holland and the Austrian Netherlands were united to form the Kingdom of the Netherlands; Prussia and Baden obtained some French provinces along the Rhine; and, in Italy, the states of Sardinia, Savoy and Genoa were united to form the Kingdom of Piedmont. As a final guarantee of peace and stability, Louis XVIII was placed on the French throne.

In 1827 the British fleet went to the aid of the Greeks in their fight to gain independence from the Turkish Empire.

The Congress System

At Vienna, 'the High Contracting Parties'—the governments of Russia, Austria, Prussia and Britain—agreed 'to renew their meetings at fixed periods.' The Great Powers were determined to prevent revolutions and to maintain the balance of power. In 1818, France joined the 'Congress System' and all seemed to be well. However, when uprisings took place in various parts of Europe in 1820, the Congress System collapsed. The Continental powers wanted to send their armies into the disturbed areas to stamp out the disorders, but Britain refused to agree, arguing that each state's integrity should be respected.

Relations deteriorated still further when the Greeks rose in revolt against the Turks in 1827. The British favoured their demands for independence but the Prussians and Austrians feared that the Greek rising would encourage subject people all over Europe to follow suit. The British Foreign Minister complained, 'Things are getting back to a wholesome state again—every nation for itself and God for us all!'

The call for reform

Britain herself was not free from the fear of revolution. The Radicals called for thorough reforms which many members of the upper classes feared would mean the end of their power and influence. On 21 July

In the Peterloo Massacre of 1819, the Manchester and Salford Yeomanry killed 11 unarmed civilians; a further 600 were injured.

1819, the Manchester and Salford Yeomanry, which largely consisted of middle-class part-time soldiers, attacked a peaceful political meeting at St Peter's Fields, Manchester, on the pretext that a riot was about to take place. An eyewitness wrote: 'Their [the cavalry's] sabres were plied to hew a way through naked held-up hands and defenceless heads. Chopped limbs and wound-gaping skulls were seen; and groans and cries were mingled with the din of that horrid confusion.' Eleven people were killed and 600 injured during the 'Peterloo Massacre'.

The unhappy state of English society was underlined by the Last Labourers' Revolt in 1830, the riots that took place before the Great Reform Act was passed in 1832, and the disturbances that followed the enforcement of the Poor Law Amendment Act of 1834. Members of the working classes began to demand the right to vote in general elections. In 1836, the Chartist Movement got under way and in 1838 a People's Charter was published calling for universal male suffrage,

The ill-fated Chartist uprising in Newport, Wales. Four thousand Chartists marched on the town, only to be dispersed by thirty soldiers.

equal constituencies, annually elected parliaments, payment for MPs, the abolition of the property qualification for MPs, and the introduction of secret balloting (voting) at general elections. In 1839, the upper and middle classes feared that the Chartists would rise in revolt. At the last moment, however, the majority of the Chartist leaders had second thoughts and withdrew their support. Unfortunately, the news of their change of heart did not reach John Frost and the Chartists of South Wales; four thousand of them marched on the town of Newport, only to be routed by thirty soldiers. Many of the Chartists were arrested and imprisoned for their part in the 'lost revolution'.

Even though the Chartists received little help or support from the middle classes at that time, the attitudes of well-to-do merchants, industrialists and professional men like doctors and engineers were changing. Many accepted Liberalism, and believed, at least in theory, in political freedom, fair taxation, basic education for all and freedom from censorship. In fact, they had come to accept many of the 'dangerous' ideas put forward by the French revolutionaries. They had seen that change was possible and even beneficial. As a result, an atmosphere slowly

Sir Robert Peel declared himself to be in favour of 'the correction of proved abuses and the redress of real grievances'.

Giuseppe Mazzini, the Italian patriot who in 1848 was to become the leader of the short-lived Roman Republic.

grew up in favour of reform. In Britain, for instance, Sir Robert Peel, the leader of the Tory Party, persuaded his conservative followers to accept the idea of change in the Tamworth Manifesto of 1834:

> If the spirit of the Reform Bill implies merely a careful review of institutions, civil and ecclesiastical, undertaken in a friendly temper, combining with the firm maintenance of established rights the correction of proved abuses and the redress of real grievances—in that case I can for myself and my colleagues undertake to act in such a spirit and with such intentions.

Indeed, it has been suggested that during the second half of the nineteenth century the Conservative Party passed at least as many important reforms improving the life of ordinary people as the Liberals.

While Peel was calling for the reform of 'proved abuses', nationalism was spreading through many European countries. The supporters of nationalism believed that subject peoples everywhere had the right to independence. Giuseppe Mazzini, the great Italian patriot, wrote:

'A nation is an association of all those who are brought together by language, by given geographical conditions or by the role assigned them by history.' The French revolutionary armies had fostered the growth of these ideas wherever they went.

Revolution in Europe

In 1830, a series of revolutions threatened the stability of Europe. Charles X of France was forced to abdicate and Louis Philippe, the son of the Duke of Orleans, was elected King of the French by the Chamber of Deputies. The Belgians rose in revolt against the Dutch and managed to obtain their independence with the help of the French and British. Elsewhere nationalists were not so lucky: the Poles tried to drive out their Russian overlords, but were crushed; and the Italians tried to overthrow their Austrian masters but found their military strength too much for them.

Once again, the ruling classes in most European countries had managed to hold on to their power. It remained to be seen whether they would try to satisfy the demands of the liberals and nationalists or seek to suppress them.

In the most successful of the uprisings of 1830, the Belgian people rose against their Dutch masters and gained independence.

9 THE YEAR OF REVOLUTIONS, 1848

Even though in 1830 the traditional rulers of Europe, with the exception of the King of the Netherlands, had managed to retain power, the strength of the nationalist and liberal movements was growing. Social problems had been ignored rather than remedied, and by 1848 Europe was ripe once more for revolution.

France

As on previous occasions, France provided the spark. Louis Philippe had proved to be an ineffective king. The urban and rural workers were deeply dissatisfied: wages were low, prices high. In this atmosphere, Socialism appeared. Saint-Simon, one of its authors, wrote:

Saint-Simon, a leading French socialist thinker, who coined the slogan, 'from each according to his capacity, to each according to his work'.

Louis Philippe, who had come to the French throne in the rising of 1830, was forced to abdicate, and went into exile in 1848.

'The immediate purpose of my enterprise is to improve as much as possible the conditions of the class which has no means of livelihood but the labour of its hands. My purpose is to improve the conditions of this class not only in France, but in England, Belgium, Portugal, Spain, Italy, and in the rest of Europe.'

Louis Blanc, a journalist, suggested that 'The chief object [of working-class reform] is to allow the worker to enjoy the fruits of his work; to restore those whom poverty degrades to the dignity of human nature; to enlighten those whose intelligence, for want of education, is but a dim lamp in the midst of darkness.'

Middle-class liberals, led by Louis Thiers, demanded parliamentary reform. Thiers supported the radical working-class leaders in insisting that every man should be allowed to vote in general elections. He organized a series of Reform Banquets to unite public opinion and force the government to take action. When the National Guard refused to move against demonstrators, Thiers' followers seized government offices and Louis Philippe abdicated. The Second Republic was set up, although its life was short: Louis Napoleon, a relative of the great Bonaparte, was elected President and eventually got himself recognized as Napoleon III.

Chartism

'The effect [of the French Revolution] was electrical,' an English Chartist wrote. 'Frenchmen, Germans, Poles, Magyars [Hungarians] sprang to their feet, embraced and shouted in the wildest enthusiasm. Snatches of oratory [speeches] were delivered in excited tones, and flags were taken from the walls, to be waved exultantly, amidst cries of "Vive la République".' The Chartist leaders contemplated overthrowing the government. During the ensuing emergency, the old Duke of Wellington was placed in charge of the defence of London and enlisted the help of anybody who could be trusted. 'All the clerks and others in the different [government] offices', a civil servant noted, 'are ordered to be sworn in as special constables, and to constitute themselves into garrisons.' In the event, the People's Petition, or demand for reforms was sent to the Houses of Parliament in a cab. As on previous occasions, Parliament refused to consider the petition and Chartism died as a political force, although most of its ideals survived and were realized in years to come.

As on previous occasions, the Chartists' petition of 1848 was ignored by Parliament, and the Chartist movement collapsed.

Europe in revolt

More dramatic risings took place in Italy. Milan and Venice were seized by nationalists; Charles Albert, the King of Piedmont, declared war on Austria; the Pope fled from Rome and a Roman Republic was set up, with Giuseppe Garibaldi and his Legionaries as its defenders and Mazzini as its leader. However, the Austrians and the other reactionary powers were too strong for Charles Albert. He was defeated and forced to abdicate in favour of his son, Victor Emmanuel II. The Roman Republic was destroyed in 1849, although twelve years later the work started in 1848 was completed by Garibaldi, Count Cavour and Victor Emmanuel II when the new Kingdom of Italy was established.

Garibaldi was passionately devoted to the cause of a united Italy; although unsuccessful in 1848, he was to help bring the Kingdom of Italy into being in 1861.

News of Louis Philippe's downfall in France sparked off demonstrations in Vienna, the Hapsburg capital, which forced Metternich's resignation.

In March 1848, rebels seized control of Vienna, the capital of the Hapsburg Empire. The Emperor Ferdinand had an epileptic fit, and Prince Alfred von Windischgrätz, who believed that 'human beings begin at barons' pleaded to be made dictator so that he could shoot down the students and workers. Prince Metternich, who for years had dominated not only Austria but European affairs generally, was dismissed and fled for his life. Free speech was granted and a National Guard set up. However, the upper and middle classes quickly lost their enthusiasm for reform when they realized how radical the changes the workers wanted were, and in October the rising was crushed by the army.

Meanwhile, in Budapest, the Hungarians rose in a revolt led by Louis Kossuth. Bowed down by worry the Emperor Ferdinand granted them a constitution. All was well until October, by which time Ferdinand had recovered control in Austria. He immediately dissolved the Hungarian Assembly and placed a military ruler in command. In their fury at the Emperor's treachery, the Hungarians again rose in revolt. The Emperor was persuaded to abdicate in favour of his eighteen-year-old nephew Francis Joseph, who ruled the Hapsburg Empire until his death in 1916. Francis Joseph placed an able and ruthless soldier, Marshal Radetzky, in charge of his armies and the Hungarian rebels were swept to defeat. A Czech rising suffered the same fate.

Even Prussia experienced a severe crisis. Riots in Berlin forced Frederick William IV to grant a constitution. An attempt was even made to unite the whole of Germany by setting up a National Assembly

64

at Frankfurt. However, as Karl Marx, the founder of Communism, sneered, 'It was an assembly of old women.' While the delegates wasted their time in fruitless debate, Frederick William withdrew from his capital, reorganized his army and stamped out the rising. The German nationalists had to wait until 1871 for Otto von Bismarck to unite Germany in the name of Prussia.

Despite the widespread nature of the uprisings, 1848, the year of revolutions, produced little in the way of gains for ordinary people. Only the French succeeded in changing their form of government, and they promptly exchanged their republic for Louis Napoleon's 'Second Empire'. However, the nationalist movements in Italy and Germany had been strengthened and were to realize their aims within a few years. Even the Hapsburgs attempted to meet the wishes of some of their subject peoples by dividing their empire in two and giving the Hungarians self-government. This was an improvement but it hardly satisfied the desires of all the other peoples, who had to wait until total defeat in the First World War led to the disintegration of the once-mighty empire.

Louis Napoleon, President of France from 1848 to 1852, and subsequently, as Napoleon III, its emperor and dictator.

The birth of Communism

Like all great moments in history, 1848 can be seen as a beginning rather than an end. This was the year in which Karl Marx (with Friedrich Engels) first published *The Communist Manifesto*. In it he proclaimed, 'The immediate aim of the Communists is the same as that of all the other proletarian [urban working-class] parties: formation of the proletariat into a class, overthrow of the bourgeois [middle-class, capitalistic] supremacy, conquest of political power by the proletariat.' He went on to outline the main points of his policy:

The Communist Manifesto *first appeared in 1848. At the time few people read it, and it played no part in bringing about the uprisings of that year.*

Manifest

der

Kommunistischen Partei.

Veröffentlicht im Februar 1848.

Proletarier aller Länder vereinigt euch.

London.

Gedruckt in der Office der „Bildungs=Gesellschaft für Arbeiter"
von J. E. Burghard.
46, LIVERPOOL STREET, BISHOPSGATE.

1. Abolition of property in land
2. A heavy progressive or graduated income tax
3. Abolition of all right of inheritance
4. Confiscation of the property of all emigrants and rebels
5. Centralization of credit in the hands of the State
6. Centralization of the means of communication and transport
7. Extension of factories and instruments of production owned by the State
8. Equal liability of all to work
9. Combination of agriculture with manufacturing industry
10. Free education for all children in public (State) schools

Most people at the time who read the 'Manifesto' regarded it as the ravings of a madman. And yet, in the twentieth century, it is the most talked about and debated text in the political world.

The 1848 revolutions failed, as Engels pointed out, because the middle class 'inclines towards liberalism when the bourgeoisie is in the ascendant; it has fits of democratic fervour as soon as the bourgeoisie has established its own supremacy, but subsides into profound discouragement as soon as the class below it, the proletariat, attempts independent action.' Although the peoples of Europe wanted liberty, they rose before the social and economic structures inherited from the *ancien régime* had weakened sufficiently. However, the foundations had been laid for the great advance of the nationalists, liberals and working classes during the years before the First World War inaugurated another age of revolution.

Karl Marx (on the left) with his family, and his close friend and collaborator Friedrich Engels.

GLOSSARY

Bourgeoisie   The moneyed middle classes.

Chartists   Members of the working classes who demanded the vote and right to take a full part in the political life of their country.

Clipper   A fast, narrow, sharp-prowed sailing ship with a deep keel to reduce lateral movement through the water.

Coalition   A military alliance between a number of countries for their mutual defence or to attack a common enemy.

Communists   Extreme Socialists who believe that revolution is necessary to destroy the bourgeoisie and create a classless society.

Conservatives   Members of a British political party, pledged to support the monarchy, the Church of England and other British institutions, and which believes in reforming 'proved abuses'.

Enclosures   The reorganization of huge medieval open fields into smaller, compact fields bordered by hedges or walls.

Executive   The part of the government that sees that policies, laws and decisions are carried out.

Feudal system   A pyramidal organization of society into landowners, the 'upper classes' and producers, the 'lower classes'.

Gentry   Rich, large-scale landowners of high social class but without titles of nobility.

Great Powers   The most powerful nations, including France, Austria, Prussia, Russia and Britain.

Jacobins   Extreme French revolutionaries who wished to establish a republic.

Liberals   Politicians who believe in equality of opportunity, political freedom, fair taxation and a programme of reforms to ensure that everybody enjoys at least a minimum standard of living.

Nationalists   Those who believe that members of the same race/cultural group/nationality should be allowed to rule themselves and live according to their own beliefs, values and customs.

Philosophes   Eighteenth-century thinkers who believed that life was controlled by laws which could be discovered by reasoning.

Reducing   Separating a metal from its ore by a chemical process.

Revolution   A political, economic, social or artistic 'upheaval' which brings about wide-ranging changes in the existing situation.

Rotation   A system of land use which involves changing the crops grown on land from year to year in order to maintain the chemical balance of the soil and crop yields.

Shuttle   A large needle or bobbin which carries the weft (horizontal threads) between the warp (the vertical threads) in weaving.

Socialists   Those who believe that the people as a whole should own the means of production, distribution and communication.

Spinning   The production of yarn or thread for the weaving industry.

States General   The ancient French parliament which consisted of three 'estates' or houses: the aristocracy, clergy and bourgeoisie.

Suspension bridge   A bridge held up by flexible supports passing over a tower or support at each end.

Turnpike   A carefully prepared and maintained road which passengers paid a small fee to use.

Underemployment   A situation in which labourers receive insufficient work throughout the year to maintain their own well-being and that of their families.

Weaving   The making of cloth by passing horizontal threads (weft) through vertical threads (warp).

Yeomanry   A force of volunteer cavalry, consisting largely of country gentlemen and farmers.

DATE CHARTS

Wars and Revolutions

1755–1783	The American War of Independence
1789	French Revolution begins
1792–97	The War of the First Coalition
1798–99	Napoleon's Egyptian campaign
1799–1802	The War of the Second Coalition
1805	The War of the Third Coalition
1806	The Continental System
1806–7	The War of the Fourth Coalition
1813–14	The War of Liberation
1814–15	The Congress of Vienna
1815	The Hundred Days
1820	Risings in Portugal, Spain & Naples
1830	The Warsaw uprising
1848	Risings in Vienna, Hungary, Prussia and Italy

Industry, Transport and Agriculture

Date	Cotton	Iron
1701		
1709		Coke for furnaces (Darby of Coalbrookdale)
1711		
1733	Kay's Flying Shuttle (weaving)	
1742		Crucible steel (Benjamin Huntsman)
1761		
1764	Hargreaves' Spinning Jenny	
1766		
1769	Arkwright's Water Frame (spinning)	
1777		
1779	Crompton's Mule (spinning)	
1784		Cort's Puddling Process
1785	Cartwright's Power Loom (weaving)	
1793		
1800		
1802		
1803		
1825		
1829		
1838		
1845		

Steam	Transport	Agriculture
Denis Papin		Tull's Seed Drill
Thomas Savery	Turnpike Trusts	
Newcomen's		
Atmospheric Engine.		
		Tull's *Horse*
		Hoeing Husbandry
	Road builders:	Townshend's
	Metcalf	Norfolk Rotation.
	Telford	
	MacAdam	
	Bridgwater Canal	
Watt's Steam		
Engine.		
	Grand Trunk Canal	
		Coke & Bakewell
		Board of Agriculture
		founded.
Maudsley's Screw		
Cutting Lathe.		
Symington's *Charlotte*		
Dundas		
	Trevithick's locomotive	
	Stockton–Darlington	
	Railway.	
	Stephenson's *Rocket*	
Sirius		
Brunel's *Great*	Clipper Ships	
Britain		

The Arts and Architecture

Date	Painting	Architecture
1750		Walpole's Strawberry Hill (1750–70)
	Gainsborough's *Watering Place* (1777)	
	Stubbs' *Anatomy of the Horse* (1786)	
		Bank of England (1795–1827)
1800	David's *Napoleon at The Great St Bernard Press* (1801)	
	Turner's *Sun Rising in a Mist* (1807)	Regent Street (1811)
	Goya's *Disasters of War* (1810)	Brighton Pavilion (1815–1823)
	Constable's *Haywain* (1821)	Pugin's *Gothic Ornaments* (1831)
	Delacroix's *Liberty Guiding the People* (1830)	
		Houses of Parliament (Barry & Pugin 1836–1852)
	Turner's *The Fighting Temeraire* (1839)	
	J. Ruskin's *Modern Painters* (1843)	
	Pre-Raphaelite Brotherhood founded (1848)	Street's Law Courts (1866)

Literature	Poetry	Music
	Gray's *Elegy* (1751)	
		Mozart's *Magic Flute* (1791)
	Crabbe's *Village* (1783)	Haydn's 'Surprise' Symphony (1791)

Literature	Poetry	Music
	Wordsworth & Coleridge's *Lyrical Ballads* (1798)	Beethoven's 'Pathetique' Sonata (1799)
		Beethoven's 'Moonlight' Sonata (1802)
	Wordsworth's *Prelude* (1805)	Beethoven's 'Eroica' Symphony (1804)
Scott's *Marmion* (1808)	Byron's *English Bards & Scots Reviewers* (1809)	
Austen's *Sense and Sensibility* (1811)		Schubert's *Gretchen am Spinnrade* (1814)
	Coleridge's *Kubla Khan* (1816) Shelley's *Revolt of Islam* (1817)	Schubert's *Earl King* (1816)
Scott's *Ivanhoe* (1820)		
Cobbett's *Rural Rides* (1830)	Heine's Poems (1821)	Mendelssohn's *A Midsummer Night's Dream* (1826)
Dickens' *Pickwick Papers* (1836–7)	Tennyson's *Lady of Shalott* (1832)	
		Schumann's Piano Concerto in A Minor (1841) R. Wagner's *Flying Dutchman* (1843)
A. Dumas' *The Count of Monte Cristo* (1844)		
C. Bronte's *Jane Eyre* (1847)		Liszt's 'Preludes' (1845)
E. Bronte's *Wuthering Heights* (1847)		Mendelssohn's *Elijah* (1846)
E. Gaskell's *Mary Barton* (1848)		

FURTHER READING

Addy, J. *The Agrarian Revolution* Longman, 1968
Addy, J. *A Coal and Iron Community in the Industrial Revolution* Longman, 1970
Addy, J. and Power, E. *The Industrial Revolution* Longman, 1976
Barlow, M. E. *The Foundations of Modern Europe, 1789–1871* Bell, 1968
Campling, E. and J. *The French Revolution* Batsford, 1984
Droz, J. *Europe between Revolutions 1815–1848* Fontana, 1967
The Editors of Horizon Magazine *The French Revolution* Cassell, 1965
Harris, N. *Spotlight on the Industrial Revolution* Wayland, 1985
Johnson, D. *The French Revolution* Wayland, 1970
Lewis, G. *Life in Revolutionary France* Batsford, 1972
Pizzinelli, L. M. *Robespierre* Hamlyn, 1968
Power, E. *A Textile Community in the Industrial Revolution* Longman, 1969
Rudé, G. *Revolutionary Europe, 1783–1815* Fontana, 1964
Searby, P. *The Chartists* Longman, 1967
Symonds, R. *Britain, Europe and the World, 1714–1848* Heinnemann, 1975
Watson, R. *Edwin Chadwick, Poor Law and Public Health* Longman, 1969
Wright, D. G. *Revolution and Terror in France, 1789–1785* Longman, 1974

PICTURE ACKNOWLEDGEMENTS

The illustrations in this book were supplied by: The British Museum 4; Mary Evans Picture Library *front cover*, 34, 39, 41, 54, 55, 56, 58, 59, 60, 62, 64; The Guildhall Library 47; The Mansell Collection 7, 23, 50, 52, 53, 63; The National Maritime Museum, London 17, 44; The National Portrait Gallery 48, 57; Peter Newark's Historical Pictures 12, 13, 18, 29, 61, 65; Peter Newark's Western Americana 8; Nottingham Public Libraries 49; Ann Ronan Picture Library 32, 37, 38, 40; The Science Museum 9, 26, 31, 35, 43, 45; the Tate Gallery, London 46; University of Reading, Institute of Agricultural History and Museum of English Rural Life 24, 25, 27, 28; Malcolm S. Walker 6. The remaining pictures are from the Wayland Picture Library.

INDEX